The amazing me!

Now that the kids are gone...

Daphne Lancaster and Julia Meder

City of Oaks
Publishing

www.cityofoakspublishing.com

ISBN: 978-1-944260-01-9

Printed in the United States

Beautiful Mother,

You have loved patiently,
nurtured
and given wings for flight.
Trust
that you have given enough.

It is now your turn
to dream
and take flight
in the bright and sunny sky.

Where do you want to go?

A new journey is beginning.

In the end...
I am the only one
who can give
my children
a happy mother
who loves life.

Janene Wolsey Baadsgaard

What gifts have you given your children to move forward in the world?

Your children
will become
what you are;
so be
what you want them
to be.

David Bly

What dreams did you postpone to raise your family?

Life is change.
Growth is optional.
Choose wisely.

Albert Einstein

Remember the time when you were a young adult. Reflect on the relationship with your parents.

So I close my eyes
to old ends
and open my heart to
new beginnings.

Nick Frederickson

What would you like to discover in the world now?

It takes courage
to grow up
and become
who you really are.

EE Cummings

Describe the person you want to be.

I am not afraid of storms
for I am learning
how to sail my ship.

Louisa May Alcott

What would you need to believe about yourself to become the person you want to be?

The beauty you see in
me is a reflection of you.

Rumi

What relationships do you want to build at this time?

I alone can't
change the world,
but I can cast a stone
across the waters
to create many ripples.

Mother Theresa

How will those relationships honor who you are?

At the end of the day,
the only questions
I will ask myself are...
Did I love enough?
Did I laugh enough?
Did I make a difference ?

Katrina Mayer

What have you learned about yourself while raising your children?

The key to happiness
is letting each situation
be what it is
instead of
what you think
it should be.

Mandy Hale

What is a positive mantra for this time in your life? Why?

It is never too late to be
what you might have been.

George Eliot

How do you enjoy your role in the life of your adult child?

Six
months
later

It's not what you do for
your children,
but what you have taught
them to do for themselves,
that will make them
successful human beings.

Ann Landers

What can you believe about the abilities that lie within your child that will help them impact in the world?

I always wonder
why birds stay in the
same place
when they can fly
anywhere on the earth.
Then I ask myself
the same question.

Harun Yahya

What plans and dreams are you making now for yourself?

Happiness cannot be
traveled to, owned,
earned, worn
or consumed.
Happiness is the spiritual
experience of living
every minute with love,
grace, and gratitude.

Denis Waitley

Considering what brings you happiness, how do you see your new self moving forward?

To be beautiful
means to be yourself.
You don't need to be
accepted by others.
You need to accept
yourself.

Thich Nhat Hanh

Describe the person you are becoming.
Remember to use beautiful words.

The biggest change
for me as a mom
was realizing I needed to
put someone else
before me.
Now the hardest part
about the empty nest
is learning
to put myself first.

Kim Alexis

What do you love about yourself today, and what other parts of yourself do you want to discover?

Life is a balance of
holding on and letting go.

Rumi

Which relationships have brought you joy, and which relationships are you still working on building?

Make each day
your masterpiece.

John Wooden

How have those relationships helped you to grow?

The question isn't who's
going to let me;
it's who is going to stop me.

Ayn Rand

What have you learned about yourself during this time of re-defining yourself?

Life is not measured by
the number of breaths
we take, but by
the moments that take
our breath away.

Maya Angelou

How are you living the mantra you gave yourself 6 months ago?
See page 53.

What is done in love
is done well.

Vincent Van Gogh

What do you want your role to look like in the life of your young adult?

You are never too old to
set another goal or to
dream a new dream.

C.S. Lewis

Reflect on your vision and dreams for your future.

More journals from City of Oaks Publishing

Creating guided journals for you to write about the adventures in your life is the heart of what we do. These journals can serve a multitude of needs – a canvas for self-discovery; a conversation starter or encouragement for reflection, a memory book to cherish or even a guide to get out there and start living!

Visit us on www.cityofoakspublishing.com - for news, freebies and more!

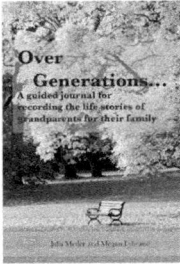

Over Generations
Great for a gift and perfect as a conversation starter for families, the Over Generations guided journal can help you capture important memories for future generations. Use this journal as a memory book to preserve your family history.

The Sound of Revival
This collection of timeless hymns includes thought-provoking journal questions to inspire readers to strengthen their walk with God. By focusing on one classic hymn each week, readers are taken on a yearlong journey of self-discovery and reflection on the enduring nature of God.

How to Get Your Groove Back
Are you going through a break-up and struggling to work through a jumble of emotions? This 6-week journal can help guide you through that emotional turmoil and help you establish a path for brighter days ahead.

The Journes to Yourself
Good coaching will lead you to your true authentic self. You made the decision to invest in yourself and your development when you started your coaching. To get the most out of your coaching sessions it helps to write your thoughts about it down. This journal covers twelve coaching sessions.

And more journals from City of Oaks Publishing

Moving Up!

With practical advice and a workbook to help you plan and record logistics and details, the Moving Up journal guides you through the critical first months of starting a new job.